Joey

A Baby Koala and His Mother

NIC BISHOP

SCHOLASTIC INC.

Deep in
the gum
tree
forest,

Joey sleeps in his mother's arms.

He wakes up.

Today is a new day.

He wriggles and squirms.

Joey is very hungry.

It is time for breakfast.

He wants Mom
to wake up.

But Mom is
still sleeping.

Joey needs to go and get food.
He has an idea!

Feeling big, Joey crawls right over his mom.

But she still wants to sleep.

Joey reaches
a branch
with yummy
gum tree
leaves.

He nibbles a bit.

Suddenly, he hears a noise!

Joey hurries back.

He is now safe with his mom.

But she
still wants
to sleep.

He tries to
wake her.

He scratches
her ear.

He climbs
on her head.

But Mom
is not ready
to wake up.

It has been a busy morning for Joey.

He falls asleep.

Mom opens
her eyes.

Joey wakes
up, too!

Mama carries Joey
high into the
gum trees.

Finally it is time for breakfast.

Joey munches and munches and munches.

author's note

Koalas are found in Australia. They live in tall forests of eucalyptus trees, which are also called gum trees. Koalas are marsupials, like kangaroos, and raise their young in a special pouch, called a marsupium. A baby is called a joey. When born, it is the size of a jelly bean and it must climb through its mother's fur to reach the pouch. There it will stay warm and safe, drinking its mother's milk and growing bigger. Muscles keep the pouch closed so the joey does not fall out.

After a few months, the joey peeks out of the pouch to eat a type of green gooey droppings, called pap, that its mother makes. This is like baby food and gives the joey the bacteria it will need in its gut to digest eucalyptus leaves later on.

The joey will leave the pouch for the first time when it is about six months old. Soon it will start to ride on its mother's back, like the joey in this book, and explore nearby. It will eat eucalyptus leaves as well as drink milk from its mother.

Eucalyptus leaves are tough to eat. They are chewy and have toxins that the koala must break down. It is no wonder that koalas like only the tastiest leaves. They often sniff them first to check them out. Their favorite leaves are the young ones at the tips of branches. These provide enough moisture so that a koala rarely needs to drink. But a koala's leafy diet provides such little energy that it sleeps for about eighteen hours a day. That means a lively joey can get bored waiting for its mother to wake up.

When it is about twelve months old, a joey is able to start looking after itself. It will often feed close to its mother for another year or so before moving away into the forest. A koala will live for ten to fifteen years in the wild.

ISBN 978-1-338-73026-5

12 11 10 9 8 7 6 5 4 3 2 1   22 23 24 25 26 27

Printed in the U.S.A.   40

Originally published in hardcover by Scholastic Press, July 2020

This edition first printing, January 2022

The text type was set in PT Sans Narrow Bold. The display type was set in BigSmalls Bold.
Book design by Marijka Kostiw